Flightless Birds of the Sou

GW01071759

Pengu...

Flightless Birds of the Southern Hemisphere
Penguins

PART OF THE SEAWORLD EDUCATION SERIES

Research/Writing/Layout
Judith Coats

Technical Advisors
Brad Andrews
Sherry Branch
Stephanie Costelow
Tom Goff
Bill Hughes
Daniel K. Odell, Ph.D.
Jack Pearson
Wendy Turner
Dudley Wigdahl

Education Directors
Lorna Crane
Hollis J. Gillespie
Bob Mindick
Joy L. Wolf

Editorial Staff
Jody Byrum
Judith Coats
Deborah Nuzzolo
Donna Parham

Illustration
Doug Fulton

Photos
Mike Aguilera
Bob Couey
Lauren DuBois
Minden Pictures
  Fred Bavendam
  Frans Lanting
  Tui de Roy
  Konrad Wothe
SeaWorld San Diego and
  SeaWorld Orlando Photo
  Departments
Frank S. Todd
Rob Yordi

Photographs

Cover: Emperor penguins (*Aptenodytes forsteri*) slide in the snow.
Title page: Adélie penguins (*Pygoscelis adeliae*) plunge into the sea.
Page 1: An Adélie penguin swims by in an underwater closeup.
Pages 10-11: Unidentified penguins porpoising at sea.
Pages 22-23: African penguins (*Spheniscus demerus*) walk on the beach.
Pages 36-37: The feather crests of rockhopper penguins (*Eudyptes chrysocome*) get a lift from the wind.
Pages 74-75: Adélie penguins watch as a cruise ship glides by an iceberg.

©2001 Sea World, Inc. All Rights Reserved.

Published by the SeaWorld San Diego Education Department
500 Sea World Drive, San Diego, California, 92109-7904

No part of this publication may be reproduced or transmitted in any form or by any means without permission in writing from the publisher.

ISBN 1-893698-05-X
Printed in the United States of America

CONTENTS

Meet the Penguins

"Penguins are unquestionably unique and exotic birds...so distinctive in appearance and behavior that they are almost never confused with any other bird—or for that matter, any other animal."

Frank Todd

Adélie penguins portray the
"typical" penguin.

W ho hasn't chuckled at the comical sight of a penguin
waddling to and fro across the ice? Penguin characters adorn
merchandise, clothing, books, and film. But like the adage "Don't
judge a book by its cover," penguins are not funny little animals
dressed up in tuxedos. These birds are serious survivors that can
thrive in planet Earth's most extreme weather, from the sweltering
tropics to the frozen South Pole.

 ## What is a Penguin?

P enguins are birds. All birds belong to the scientific class Aves.
Birds possess an outer covering of feathers, lay eggs, and have
warm blood and front limbs modified as wings. The specialized
adaptations of penguins set them apart from other birds; penguins
comprise their own order (Sphenisciformes) and family
(Spheniscidae).

The origin of the word "penguin" has long been debated.
Researchers' and historians' theories range from references to the
amount of fat penguins possess (*penguigo* in Spanish and *pinguis* in
Latin) to the claim that the word was derived from two Welsh
words (*pen gwyn*) meaning *white head*. The most agreed-upon
explanation is that "penguin" was used as a name for the now-
extinct great auk, which modern-day penguins resemble and
for which they were once mistaken.

2

Most scientists recognize 17 species of penguins in six genera.

Aptenodytes includes the emperor (*A. forsteri*) and the king (*A. patagonicus*): the two largest penguins.

Pygoscelis includes the Adélie (*P. adeliae*), the gentoo (*P. papua*), and the chinstrap (*P. antarctica*) penguins. Often called "brush-tailed" penguins, these medium-sized birds have long, stiff tail feathers.

Eudyptes includes the rockhopper (*E. chrysocome*), the macaroni (*E. chrysolophus*), the royal (*E. schlegeli*), the Fiordland crested (*E. pachyrhynchus*), the erect-crested (*E. sclateri*), and the Snares Island (*E. robustus*) penguins. All these penguins have bright, long, head feathers and are referred to as "crested" penguins.

Spheniscus includes the Magellanic (*S. magellanicus*), the Humboldt (*S. humboldti*), the African (*S. demersus*), and the Galápagos (*S. mendiculus*) penguins. These penguins live in the warm weather of the tropics or subtropics.

Megadyptes includes only the yellow-eyed penguin (*M. antipodes*).

Eudyptula includes the fairy or little blue penguin (*E. minor*), the smallest of all penguins. Some scientists recognize an additional species: the white-flippered penguin, *Eudyptula albosignata*, which closely resembles the fairy penguin.

Penguins in the genus Eudyptes, like the rockhopper penguin, have brightly colored, long head feathers.

3

The closest living relatives to penguins are the albatrosses, shearwaters, and petrels (order Procellariiformes), and loons and grebes (order Gaviiformes). DNA studies also suggest a relationship with the frigatebirds (order Pelecaniformes).

Penguin Homes

All penguins live south of the equator. Well, almost all. Some Galápagos penguins living on Isla Isabela nest a few miles north of the equator. Penguins have populated the shores of every continent in the Southern Hemisphere—South America, Africa, Australia, and Antarctica—in addition to the numerous islands of the Southern Ocean. Climate extremes range from the very cold shores of Antarctica to the hot sands on African beaches. Generally, penguin populations concentrate on islands and remote continental shorelines that are free of land predators and have nutrient-rich, cold-water currents that provide an abundant food supply.

While on land, some penguins gather in the thousands, like this Adélie penguin colony on Paulet Island off the tip of the Antarctic Peninsula. Most penguins travel alone or in small groups while at sea.

In general, penguin populations are defined geographically. Beginning at the South Pole, only two penguins, the emperor and the Adélie, live year-round on the land and in the seas surrounding the Antarctic continent. Moving north, gentoo and chinstrap penguins nest along the relatively warmer and seasonally ice-free Antarctic Peninsula.

The greatest number of penguin species (12) live between 45° and 60°S latitude. This area includes the islands of the Southern Ocean including New Zealand, and the tips of South America and Australia. The greatest penguin diversity occurs around the mainland and islands of southern New Zealand. The Fiordland crested, yellow-eyed, fairy, Snares Island, erect-crested, and royal penguins live here. Another highly populated area is the tip of South America: around the Falkland Islands live the king, rockhopper, gentoo, and macaroni penguins. Off the west coast of South America are Humboldt penguins while Magellanics live off the west and east coast. The African penguin lives exclusively on the African coasts. The northernmost penguin is the Galápagos, on the Galápagos Islands.

Magellanic penguin

A Penguin's Profile

The trademark comical waddle and upright stance of penguins results from their superb adaptations to a water environment. The penguin body is fusiform (tapered toward each end) with a large head, short neck, and elongated body. When swimming, a penguin tucks its head into its shoulders, creating a shape that offers little resistance when moving through water. The legs and webbed feet are set far back on the body. The tail is short and wedge-shaped, with 14 to 18 stiff tail feathers. A penguin uses its tail and feet like a boat's rudder to steer in the water.

A penguin's black and white coloration is an example of countershading. When swimming in the ocean, countershading helps penguins hide. The dark dorsal (back) side blends in with the dark ocean depths when viewed from above. The light ventral (under) side blends in with the lighter surface of the sea when viewed from below. The result blends bird and environment colors so predators and prey do not see a contrast between the two.

Hearing and sight are a penguin's two most important senses. Most birds have a hearing range from 0.1 to 8.0 kHz. (Human hearing range is 0.02 to 17.00 kHz.) Although hearing for penguins has not been well researched, vocalizing has. Penguins recognize mates and chicks and communicate aggression, courtship, and other behaviors by using specific calls.

Penguins see better under water than in air. In air, penguins are nearsighted. Studies show penguins are sensitive to violet, blue, and green light; indicating the possibility of color vision.

Generally, the senses of taste and smell are poorly developed in birds. But some seabirds (albatrosses, petrels and other Procellariiforms) have larger olfactory lobes. In a study comparing the diameter of the olfactory lobe in relation to the diameter of the forebrain in 100 bird species, the snow petrel Pagodroma nivea had the largest ratio (37 percent) versus the black-capped chickadee Parus atricapillus at 3 percent. A larger olfactory lobe may indicate a more acute sense of smell. Recent research has found the olfactory lobe of a penguin's brain to be larger than most birds, suggesting that a sense of smell (chemo-reception) is more developed for penguins than earlier studies indicated.

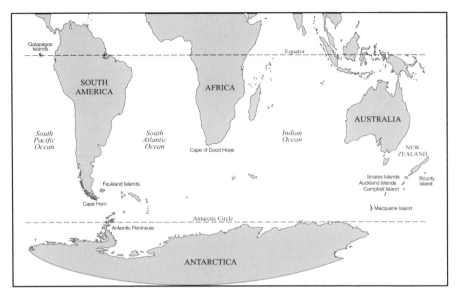

To date, all penguin fossil fragments have been found south of the Equator; in Antarctica, Australia, New Zealand, South Africa, and South America. Modern-day penguins also live south of the Equator.

 *Penguin History*

Discovery. The first European explorers to see penguins probably were part of the Portuguese expedition of Bartholomeu Dias de Novaes in 1487–88. These explorers were the first to travel around what is now known as the Cape of Good Hope in southern Africa.

Members of the Portuguese voyage of Vasco da Gama in 1497 are credited with the first documented penguin sighting. They described penguins along the southern coasts of Africa that had a "cry resembling the braying of asses." These were probably African penguins, commonly nicknamed the "jackass" penguins. The discovery of South America's Magellanic penguin was chronicled during the journey of Spanish explorer Ferdinand Magellan in 1520.

Fossil record. Scientists recognize 40 species of extinct penguins. Fossil records show that penguins probably evolved during the Cretaceous period (140–65 million years ago) from a flying ancestor. To date, the discovery of all penguin fossil fragments has been limited to the Southern Hemisphere (Antarctica, Australia, New Zealand, South Africa, and South America).

8

Thomas Huxley described and named the first penguin fossil fragments in 1859. Found in New Zealand, the fragments dated back to the Oligocene age (25 to 30 million years ago). Named *Palaeeudyptes antarcticus*, the species was estimated to stand 1.2 to 1.5 m (4–5 ft.). As of 1976, the specimen resided at the Natural History Museum, Cromwell Road in London, England.

Fossil records show some of the largest extinct species lived in the Miocene Period (11 to 25 million years ago). *Pachydyptes ponderosus* probably stood 1.4 to 1.5 m (4.5–5 ft.), more than 0.3 m (1 ft.) taller than the tallest penguin today, the emperor. Another penguin, *Anthropornis nordenskjoldi* probably stood 1.5 to 1.8 m (5–5.9 ft.). Both extinct species may have weighed between 90 and 135 kg (198–298 lb.). Scientists calculated these measurements from the large-sized flipper and leg fossil-bone fragments found in New Zealand and on Seymour Island in Antarctica.

Scientists believe that ancient penguins began disappearing about the same time that the number of prehistoric seals and small whales started increasing in the oceans. Some scientists hypothesize that seals, whales, and penguins competed for the same food sources, or that the penguins may have become prey themselves. Either or both hypotheses may explain their extinction.

Misnamed a penguin, the great auk lived on islands in the North Atlantic Ocean. Explorers searching for food easily caught and killed this large (4.5 kg or 10 lb.) flightless bird. Extensive hunting for more than 300 years caused the extinction of the great auk. The last two birds were killed in June 1844.

Masters of the Sea

"To see hundreds of penguins leaping from the sea reminds one of many leaves scattered before the wind."

Anonymous

Although penguins must come ashore to nest, lay eggs, and molt, they also spend months at sea foraging for food. Some species may spend up to 80 percent of the year at sea, never coming ashore during the nonbreeding season. Researchers have noticed barnacles growing on the tails of Fiordland crested penguins, a clear indication these birds are at sea for long periods.

Keeping Warm in Cold Water

Penguins, like all birds, are warm blooded. A healthy penguin has a body temperature range of 37.8 to 38.9°C (100–102°F). As most species of penguins swim in water that is 10°C (50°F) or less, these birds must constantly guard against heat loss. Four penguin adaptations help these birds survive; feathers, fat, metabolic rate, and blood flow.

Feathers. Penguin feathers are short, stiff, and closely spaced. In one square centimeter of skin, penguins grow about 11 feathers per square centimeter (71 per square inch), seven times more dense than a chicken's feathers. Relatively uniform in size and shape, penguin feathers have tufts of down on the feather shaft. The overlapping feather edges and tufts of down trap air between the feathers and skin. Research shows this layer of air provides 80 to 84 percent of the thermal insulation for penguins.

Penguin feathers
are short and stiff.
These feathers are
from an Adélie penguin.

Penguins that live in warmer weather—like the Magellanic (left)—have bare patches of skin around the bill and eyes to help release excess body heat. Penguins that live in cold weather—like the Adélie (right)—have feathers covering most of their bills to help conserve body heat.

Penguins often preen to keep their feathers in top condition. Like other aquatic birds, penguins have a well-developed oil gland at the base of the tail. When preening, a penguin rubs its bill across its oil gland, and then spreads the oil over its feathers. On a well-groomed penguin, water rarely touches the skin.

Fat. Penguins have a well-defined layer of fat just under the skin. This fat layer improves heat retention in cold water. Before extended fasting, a penguin's fat deposits may account for as much as 25 percent of its total body mass. In pre-breeding emperor penguins, the sub-dermal fat layer may be 2 to 3 cm (0.8–1.2 in.) thick.

Metabolic rate. But even dense feathers and a layer of fat probably are not enough to keep core body temperature stable when penguins swim and dive at sea. Studies have shown the insulative property of feathers can decrease markedly when immersed in water and compressed under pressure. Heat loss from a penguin's body increases 11 to 85 percent in water (compared with values in air), and close to 500 percent at water pressures experienced at 10 m (33 ft.). To compensate for this increased heat loss, a penguin's metabolic rate increases when at sea as compared to rates measured while ashore. For example, king penguins resting on the surface in water at -1.9°C (28°F) have a metabolic rate four times greater than in air at 0°C (32°F).

Blood flow. A penguin's circulatory system can adjust to conserve or release body heat when needed. To conserve heat, veins and arteries carrying blood to and from the flippers and legs (areas of high heat loss) are grouped close together. This close contact causes the blood traveling out to the limbs to warm the cool blood traveling into the body. Thus, blood in the feet and flippers can be cooler than the core body temperature. This countercurrent heat exchange helps ensure that heat remains in the body. If penguins become too warm, blood vessels in the skin dilate, bringing heat from within the body to the surface, where it dissipates into the air.

Other heat-saving strategies. In addition to these adaptations, penguins may also maintain body temperature by absorbing heat from the sun, especially through the black dorsal feathers. On land, penguins may huddle together to trap heat among them. Emperor and king penguins tip their toes up when resting on icy or snow-covered ground to minimize skin contact. And recent studies have shown emperor penguins are able to recapture 80 percent of heat escaping in their breath through a complex heat exchange system in their nasal passages.

Like other seabirds, penguins have internal nasal glands that help rid the body of excess salt. The secretions of very salty fluid flow down ducts to exit out the nose. The liquid collects as droplets at the tip of the bill, which penguins then shake off. These glands are so effective that penguins can drink seawater without ill effects.

Glands in the nasal passages help excrete excess salt from a penguin's blood. All penguins including this Magellanic can drink seawater without ill effects.

Penguins swim by moving their flippers in an up and down motion that resembles a flying bird's wing movement in air. Here a gentoo penguin takes a dip.

 *Flying Under Water*

The heavy, stocky penguin body is poorly shaped for flying in air but superbly adapted for movement through water. In contrast to the long, thin-boned wings of flying birds, penguin flippers have dense, broad bones with the joints of the elbows and wrists almost fused. Each flipper is covered with short, scale-like feathers. The long wing feathers typical of most birds would be too flexible for swimming through water.

To swim, penguins use their flippers in an up-and-down movement. This motion resembles the wing movements of flying birds, giving penguins the appearance of flying through the water. The penguins' solid, dense bones help counteract the buoyancy of fat and feathers. In addition, penguin wing and breast muscles are well developed to push against the dense water.

Reaching top speeds. Although swimming speeds generally are not well known, recent research has documented the swimming speeds

Galápagos penguins

Social Scene

Although well studied on land, penguin behavior at sea is relatively unknown. In general, individual penguins disperse from crowded nesting grounds to open-ocean feeding areas. Specific breeding pairs do not remain together, although 10 or more adult penguins may be seen swimming as a group. Scientists have observed African penguins flocking and feeding together at sea. When Adélie penguins gather in groups at sea, their behavior is often synchronized: individuals dive and surface at the same time.

Foraging in groups presents some advantages over solitary feeding. There is a better chance of finding prey with many individuals searching instead of just one. When prey is found, coordinating feeding behavior may allow for each individual to catch and eat more. Also, small penguins gathered together in a group may confuse or deter possible predators. This is a protective behavior similar to schools of small fish presenting a larger "image" to predators.

When feeding at sea during non-breeding months, some penguins migrate, traveling far from nesting areas. Adélies disperse and follow the formation of pack ice, traveling 150 to 650 km (94 to 403 miles) north of breeding beaches during the antarctic winter. Temperate penguins that live in milder weather, such as African or Humboldt penguins, stay close to shore even during non-breeding months. Scientists calculated that half of all non-breeding African penguins stayed within 20 km (12 miles) of the coast. The most tropical penguin, the Galápagos, remains close to the islands year-round, finding food that lives in the cold water currents surrounding the area.

Galápagos penguin feeding in shallow water, Sombrero Chino, Santiago Island, Galápagos.
Photo by Tui de Roy, Minden Pictures.

of some individual penguins. The fastest swimmers belong to the genus *Aptenodytes*. Emperors have been observed swimming 14.4 kph (8.9 mph), though they normally do not exceed 10.8 kph (6.7 mph). Both kings and chinstraps have been recorded at 8.6 kph (5.3 mph), Adélies at 7.9 kph (4.9 mph), and fairy penguins at 2.5 kph (1.6 mph). In general, penguins can maintain a steady speed of 7 to 10 kph (4.3–6.2 mph).

When at sea, penguins travel most often under water, where swimming is more energy efficient. But penguins breathe air and must come to the surface, especially when expending a lot of energy while swimming fast. To continue forward momentum and still catch a breath, penguins "porpoise"—they leap in and out of the water like dolphins or porpoises. Penguins may porpoise when

Adélie penguins appear to "fly" out of the water, easily jumping 1.8 m (6 ft.) into the air. This behavior is commonly seen when penguins come ashore onto rough or high terrain such as ice floes and rocky shorelines.

traveling long distances while migrating, when escaping predators, or when finding and catching prey. Porpoising appears common for all species except the king, African, and Galápagos. Researchers have not observed porpoising in emperor penguins.

Eating Fast Food

The fast-swimming penguins catch their meals on the run. Most penguins eat krill (a shrimplike crustacean in the family Euphausiidae), squids, and fishes. Various species of penguins have specific food preferences, which reduces competition among

Spines on the tongue and roof of the mouth (like these on this rockhopper penguin) help catch and hold slippery fish and other prey.

species. Most animals eaten by penguins live within 15.3 to 18.3 m (50–60 ft.) of the ocean's surface. The location of prey can vary seasonally and even daily.

Penguins generally stay submerged less than a minute, but gentoo and Adélie penguins often have been recorded diving under water for as long as seven minutes. The largest penguin, the emperor, feeds on midwater fishes and squids. The deepest recorded dive for an emperor penguin, which feeds on midwater fishes and squids, was 535 m (1,755 ft.), and the longest dive was 21 minutes. Obviously, these are extremes. Most observed dives are within 21 m (70 ft.) and last 2 to 8 minutes.

Penguins rely primarily on their vision while hunting. No one knows how penguins locate prey in darkness, at night, or at great depths, but some scientists hypothesize that penguins are helped by the fact that many oceanic squids, crustaceans, and fishes are bioluminescent (they produce light).

Penguins catch prey with their bills and swallow food whole while swimming. A spiny tongue and powerful jaws help grip slippery prey.

Penguins rely on the ocean for food, so when ashore, penguins don't eat. During breeding or molting seasons, fasting may last for months. Male emperor penguins fast during courtship and egg incubation and may not eat for 120 days. Before coming ashore for long periods, penguins eat heartily, building a thick fat layer that provides energy while fasting.

Chicks also may fast when they are ready to shed juvenile feathers for adult plumage. Usually by this time, the parents no longer are feeding the chick. Growth stops during this fasting period, but resumes once the molt is complete.

King penguin chicks (such as the large brown penguin in the middle) fast for up to four months—from May to August—during the antarctic winter while parents forage at sea.

21

Taking Shore Leave

"At first glance, life in a penguin community would seem to be chaotic, but there is a pattern, a kind of order."

Roger Tory Peterson

Superbly adapted to the sea, penguins must still come ashore to nest, lay eggs, and molt. Penguins usually associate in small groups while at sea, but often gather by the thousands when nesting on land. Noisy, smelly, and full of action, penguin rookeries often can be heard and smelled before being seen.

Rookery Locations

When breeding, penguins gather on land in large groups called rookeries. Rookeries are generally located near productive areas of shallow water where penguins can feed nearby. Some penguins build nests only a few yards from shore. Other species, like gentoo and king penguins, may walk as far as 3 km (1.9 mi.) inland where protected, hospitable landscape provides the best nesting areas. Macaroni and chinstrap penguins have been found nesting on rocky slopes up to 500 m (1,604 ft.) above sea level. Most penguins return to the same rookery site year after year. Studies have shown 99 percent of male Adélie penguins return to the rookery where they nested the previous year. Other penguins show

African penguins nest among rocks and low shrubs. They may collect grasses to line their nests.

24

Adélie penguins nest and rear chicks during the short antarctic summer. Strong storms in February (late summer) can increase chick mortality.

similar behavior: chinstraps were 94 percent faithful; and gentoos 63 percent faithful. There is evidence that some rookeries have been at the same site for several hundred years.

 *Nesting Material*

Depending on the species, geographic location, and the time of year, penguins nest on or in a variety of substrates. Emperor penguins breed during the antarctic winter and prefer the level surfaces of pack ice. Adélies breed during the antarctic summer and use rocky areas free of ice, sometimes traveling 50 to 60 km (31–37 mi.) from the edge of the sea ice. Chinstrap penguins nest on fairly steep slopes, while Fiordland crested penguins nest in a wet, coastal rainforest habitat. Galápagos penguins nest in volcanic caves or cracks in rock. Many of the warm-weather penguins dig burrows into the ground, or in the case of Humboldt penguins, into a deep layer of guano (bird droppings) that covers the ground.

Nesting material ranges from pebbles and small stones (Adélie and chinstrap), nearby vegetation and feathers (gentoo), to grasses and twigs (yellow-eyed). King and emperor penguins don't make nests; they incubate one egg on the tops of their feet.

Rookery Size and Density

One of the largest penguin rookeries exists on Zavodevski Island in the South Sandwich Islands group off the east coast of southern South America. Here a chinstrap rookery has been estimated at 10 million birds. Other large rookeries include estimates of 5 to 6 million rockhoppers on Beauchene Island in the Falklands and about 5 million macaronis on South Georgia Island in the South Atlantic Ocean. Author and bird illustrator Roger Tory Peterson once visited a large rookery of king penguins on South Georgia (Island). In an article for *International Wildlife*, Peterson wrote, "Even a single king penguin is impressive enough, but this profusion is an unforgettable spectacle."

A king penguin rookery like this one on South Georgia Island is crowded and noisy. Parents leave chicks ashore while feeding at sea. When they return, parents call to chicks while walking through the rookery.
Photo by Frans Lanting, Minden Pictures.

Rookery density is highest in macaroni, royal, and rockhopper penguins, with two to three breeding pairs within a square meter, only 60 to 89 cm (23–35 in.) apart. Incubating eggs on the tops of their feet, king penguins stand just out of reach of each other, avoiding the sharp jabs of their neighbors' bills. Emperors also incubate eggs on the tops of their feet. In the cold antarctic winter, incubating males huddle together for warmth. Two exceptions to colonial nesting are the yellow-eyed and Fiordland crested penguins. These birds nest far apart, up to 150 m (492 ft.) with only one to five nests every 10,000 square meters (3.8 square miles).

Breeding Behavior

Although breeding behavior varies for each species, the following sequence generally describes the seasonal activities of mating, nesting, egg laying, and chick rearing.

Coming ashore. Most penguins travel many miles from oceanic feeding areas to on-shore nesting grounds. Studies of Adélies indicate that they use the sun to navigate from sea to land. Males arrive first to the rookeries to establish and defend their nesting sites. In a study of Adélie and chinstrap penguins, females arrived one day and five days after the males, respectively.

Finding a mate. Females select males, usually choosing the same mate from the previous breeding season. Adélie penguins have been documented re-pairing with the previous year's mate 62 percent of the time. Chinstraps re-paired in 82 percent of possible cases, and gentoos re-paired 90 percent of the time. In one study of Adélies, females paired with males within minutes after their arrival.

Gentoo penguins enact the "bowing" display. This behavior appears to strengthen the bond between breeding pairs.

New mating pairs are sometimes necessary. Some males may not survive until the next breeding season, or they may return late after breeding has begun. A female may pair with a new male if her previous mate is not at the nesting site at the right time.

Courtship displays. Penguin courtship display is lively and noisy. In many species, males display first to establish a nest site and then solicit the interest of females. Not all species exhibit all displays, but in general there are three distinct types of displays.

Ecstatic. Males at the nest site commonly exhibit the ecstatic display before females arrive. The male may dip its head low then stretch its head and neck upward with flippers held outstretched and squawk or "bray." Some species, like the Adélie, chinstrap, and crested penguins, may swing their head or flap their flippers while

Male chinstrap penguins exhibit an ecstatic display.

calling. Also called trumpeting, head swinging or advertisement, this display establishes possession of a nest site, attracts females, and warns other males to stay away.

Mutual. Once paired, male and female penguins perform the mutual display together. This behavior seems to strengthen the pair bond. The mutual display is similar to the ecstatic display—head and neck stretched upward with a braying vocal. Crested, brush-tailed, and warm-weather penguins stand facing each other, performing the action in unison. Within these species there are some behavior differences. For example, gentoos generally hold their outstretched head and flippers still, while macaronis flap flippers and roll their heads from side to side. Emperor penguins have a unique display position. In their mutual display standing face to face, individuals hold their heads down with bills pointed to the

29

ground while braying. Once established, mutual displays continue throughout the breeding season, often taking place at the nest when parents switch places for egg incubation and chick feeding.

Bowing. A third common display is the bowing display. One or both penguins dips its head and points its bill at the nest or at the other bird's feet. Crested penguins may vibrate their bills while pointing in a type of bowing display called "quivering." The call is a low hiss or growl. Bowing displays may lessen the likelihood of aggression and strengthen recognition between partners.

Eggs and Chicks

In the Antarctic and Subantarctic, penguins usually mate and lay eggs in spring. Timing generally corresponds with improving weather conditions that favor successful chick raising. Eggs laid in September to November (the antarctic spring) allow chicks five to six months to grow and fledge by April, the antarctic fall. Ten of the 17 species of penguins follow this schedule: Adélies, chinstraps, gentoos (except very northern birds), rockhoppers, macaronis, royals, erect-crested, Snares Island, yellow-eyed, and Magellanics.

Emperor penguins follow a different schedule. They lay eggs in the antarctic fall, incubate them during the winter, and the eggs hatch in the spring. Chicks then fledge when food resources are the highest during the summer. Late-breeding king penguins also raise chicks this way.

Some penguins living in warmer climates have no defined season. Humboldt penguins lay eggs in all months but show two main egg-laying seasons a year, one from October to November and another from April to May. Galápagos penguins and some populations of African penguins lay eggs and raise chicks year-round, while some individuals skip breeding for an entire year.

A nest of eggs is called a clutch. With the exception of emperor and king penguins (which only lay one egg), the normal clutch has two eggs. Two-egg clutches give a better chance of at least one chick surviving.

Eggs may be white to bluish or greenish with the shape characteristic to the species. Humboldt and Adélie eggs are more or less round, while emperors and king eggs are rather pear-shaped, with one end tapering almost to a point. This pear-shaped egg fits better on top of their feet, and if it rolls off, it will roll in a circle instead of in a straight line away from the parent penguin.

Penguins lay smaller eggs relative to their body weight than almost any other bird species. From the records of SeaWorld's successful penguin breeding programs, emperor penguin eggs measure 11.1 to 12.7 cm (4.4–5 in.) long and weigh 345 to 515 g (12.1–18 oz.), about 2.3 percent of a female's body weight. Adélie penguin eggs measure 5.5 to 8.6 cm (2.2–3.4 in.) and weigh 61 to 153.5 g (2.1–5.4 oz.).

Incubating eggs. Penguins incubate eggs at approximately 36°C (96.5°F)—a bit lower for the larger emperors and kings. The smallest penguin species, the fairy penguin, has the shortest incubation period—about 33 days. Emperor penguins have the longest incubation at 62 to 66 days.

With the exception of emperor penguins, both male and female penguins take turns incubating eggs. (Male emperors do the majority of egg sitting.) Some species, like the gentoo and Magellanic, change duties daily. Others, such as the crested penguins, have

Adélie penguins (left) lay one egg in a rock lined nest. Emperor penguins (right) also lay one egg but do not build a nest. They incubate the egg on top of their feet.

A sample of penguin eggs. Clockwise from top center: king, emperor, Magellanic, Adélie, and gentoo. King and emperor penguins incubate eggs on the tops of their feet. The elliptical shape fits snugly. In addition, if the egg happens to fall off, it will roll in a circle instead of a straight line away from the parent bird.

longer shifts, sometimes with one parent sitting on the nest for 10 to 12 days at a time. Penguins, just like all incubating birds, have a featherless patch of skin that directly transfers body heat to the egg.

Mistiming between incubating parents can be fatal to unhatched chicks. If a female fails to return from a foraging trip, the male left on the nest may leave when hunger overcomes the urge to incubate eggs.

Pipping and hatching of eggs. Hatching begins with pipping: the first small hole the chick cracks in the shell. With continued movement, the chick makes larger cracks and eventually the shell falls apart. Hatching can last from 20 hours in smaller penguin species to three days for king penguins. Newly hatched chicks have only a thin covering of down feathers that may be white, gray, black, or brown. Unable to regulate its body temperature, a chick relies on its parents for warmth and protection. Depending on the species, this brooding or "guarding" phase may last up to seven weeks. Fairy penguins have the shortest (15 days) while king and emperors have the longest (30–45 days) brooding phase.

Raising chicks. Parents regurgitate half-digested fish and other food items to their chicks. In species where parents switch places at the nest often and go on daily foraging trips, chicks receive their first meal within 24 to 48 hours. For the macaroni, rockhopper, and Adélie penguins, which have longer incubation shifts, chicks may not get their first meal for five to seven days. These hardy chicks rely on yolk reserves they absorbed before hatching. Remarkably, the male emperor penguin has the ability to feed its chick, even after a 110-plus-day fast. If the female emperor does not return when the chick hatches, the male secretes a protein-rich curdlike substance from his esophagus and feeds the chick for the first few days.

The guarding or brooding phase ends when a chick has a thick coat of down feathers and is able to regulate its body temperature. Now some chicks gather in crèches. (*Crèche* is French for "childcare" or "crib.") Crèches may be loose aggregations of several chicks (macaroni, chinstrap and gentoo penguins), or crèches may be tight, large groups with all the chicks in the colony together. A crèche of king or emperor chicks may number in the thousands.

Emperor chicks (left) group together to form crèches while parents feed at sea. *Photo by Frans Lanting, Minden Pictures.*
During late chick-rearing, gentoo penguins feed chicks mostly regurgitated, half-digested fish.

Crèches provide protection from cold or windy weather and from predators like skuas, a large gull-like seabird.

Chick Survival

A chick depends on its parents for survival between hatching and the growth of its waterproof feathers. This period may range from seven weeks for Adélie chicks to 13 months for king chicks. Once a chick has fledged (replaced its juvenile down with waterproof feathers), it is able to enter the water and becomes independent of its parents.

For penguin pairs that lay two eggs, the first-laid egg is generally larger than the second, and often hatches first. This first chick usually survives while its nest mate often perishes. First-hatched chicks have the advantage of a few extra days or hours of food and growth, and can compete more successfully for food than younger siblings.

But this scenario is not true for all species. In the crested penguins (macaroni, rockhopper, and others) the second-laid egg and subsequent chick is the larger of the two; and usually the survivor. Researchers have yet to find an adequate theoretical explanation for this reversed pattern.

In yet another scenario, chinstrap, yellow-eyed, and gentoo species usually lay two eggs. Parents typically raise both chicks, which are nearly equal in size.

Life After Chicks

Once chicks fledge and leave the rookery, parent penguins need to replenish lost fat reserves. Six penguins—the Galápagos, African, Humboldt, gentoo, fairy, and yellow-eyed—forage close to shore and near the season's breeding site. Other species, especially those living in the very highest latitudes, travel farther offshore to find food. Adélie, emperor, chinstrap, and the crested penguins all migrate away from nesting areas during the non-breeding season. Migration might be caused by the extreme weather changes in Antarctica and the seasonal formation of sea ice. In addition, the location of prey items for certain penguins (fish and squid verses krill and other plankton) may necessitate migration to other areas.

Post-breeding molt. Each year penguins come ashore to molt: they shed old feathers and grow new ones. While molting, new feathers grow under the old ones, pushing them out. Because feather growth is often patchy, molting penguins look scruffy and disheveled. During this period, which may last from 13 to 34 days (Galápagos and emperor penguins respectively), penguins do not swim. The insulative properties of the feathers are lost. If penguins can't swim, then they can't feed, and so when molting, penguins fast. Before their molt, penguins eat constantly to build their fat layer, which provides energy while fasting.

While molting, penguins can look a little scruffy. This Adélie penguin has just begun to molt. In another two weeks, it will have all new feathers.

Species Spotlights

"Penguins are beautiful, interesting, and funny. They are a pleasure to watch even though they do smell and their voices are not melodious."

George Gaylord Simpson

Emperor Penguin

The largest of all penguins, the emperor penguin (*Aptenodytes forsteri*) is one of only two penguins that lives its entire life on or near the Antarctic continent. Superbly adapted to a polar environment, emperors breed on sea ice, incubate eggs during subzero weather, and can survive for four months without food. In fact, some emperors may never stand on solid land.

Emperors have striking yellow and orange patches on the sides of the neck and throat. The bill is dark purple on its sides, and the sides of the neck and throat are yellow to orange. The front is shiny white with a faint yellow hue. Sleek feathers on the head, tail, and back are bluish-black.

Emperor penguins breed and raise chicks during the antarctic winter, from egg laying in May until chick fledging in December. Main breeding grounds around the Antarctic continent include Cape Washington, Coulman Island, Victoria Island, Halley Bay, Coats Land, and Atka Bay and Dronning Maud Land. Scientists have observed colonies at 42 sites, 35 of which are active every year.

In March, emperor penguins begin to gather at the breeding site. Pair recognition begins immediately, with many birds reuniting with past mates. A study during one breeding season showed only 5 of 73 banded pairs did not reunite. Breeding reaches a peak from mid-April to early June. Females usually lay eggs between the beginning of May until mid-June.

Female emperors lay one egg, but it's the males' duty to incubate it. To transfer an egg, a pair stands face to face. The female rolls its egg from its feet to its mates', and then leaves to feed at sea. The female has not eaten for 40 days or more and has lost between 17 to 38 percent of its body weight. Males cover their eggs with a loose

AT A GLANCE

SIZE: 112 cm (44 in.), 27 to 41 kg (60–90 lb.)

DISTRIBUTION: circumpolar on antarctic continent within limits of pack ice

POPULATION: 200,000 breeding pairs

CURRENT STATUS: not globally threatened, stable with some local fluctuations that may occur naturally.

flap of abdominal skin (a brood patch). The covered eggs are warmed by direct contact with the males' skin.

By May, mostly males remain at the rookery. Egg incubation lasts 62 to 66 days, through an antarctic winter of almost total darkness and subzero temperatures. To conserve body heat, male emperors huddle in large groups, moving slowly by shuffling their feet. By late June, the females begin to return to the rookery, calling for and locating their mates. When the egg hatches, the male transfers the chick to the female and then leaves to feed at sea. Male emperors have fasted for more than four months, losing up to 50 percent of their body weight.

Chicks begin hatching in July. Newly hatched chicks have few feathers, more covering their head than body. This allows skin-to-skin contact with the parent bird and more efficient heat transfer. The well-nourished female feeds the chick regurgitated food eaten at sea. Chicks spend about six weeks in the brood patch of the parents. The males return in about 24 days, and both parents take turns feeding the chick. Foraging trips at sea may last 1 to 30 days, with the parents traveling anywhere from 164-1,454 km (102–903 miles) in a single hunting trip. A successful penguin may bring back more than 4 kg (9 lb.) of food in its stomach.

Once fully feathered in soft down, chicks congregate in large crèches. Parents call to their chicks in the crèche and the chicks respond by waddling to the edge of the group to be fed. Chicks stay in crèches from September to December. By December they have molted to their seaworthy feathers. As the ice breaks up during the Antarctic summer, the chicks ride the ice floes to open sea to feed on their own.

Adults and juveniles feed at sea, catching mainly squids, fishes, and crustaceans. Studies of diving adults have recorded depths of 535 m (1,755 ft.), one of the deepest dives of any warm-blooded animal, marine mammal or bird. Little or no light penetrates to that depth so emperors may cue in on prey by sound (vibrations in the water as prey swims by) or by spying the bioluminescent light emitted by some fishes and squids.

After breeding and raising chicks, adults molt for about a month, usually away from the breeding colony on unbroken sea-ice. The following months are spent feeding at sea, preparing for the next breeding season beginning in March.

King Penguin

The second largest of all penguin species, the king penguin (*Aptenodytes patagonicus*) is tall and sleek, with bright golden orange ear patches, a black head, and a golden breast that fades to a white underbelly. Feet are black, and the back is silvery gray-blue.

King penguins breed on most of the islands of the Southern Ocean including the Falklands, South Georgia, Marion, Prince Edward, Crozet, Kerguelen, Heard, and Macquarie.

King penguins have the longest egg-laying/chick-rearing season, taking 14 to 16 months. Because of this extended period, mating pairs successfully raise chicks only twice in three years. Generally, females lay eggs November to March, with both males and females incubating the one egg on top of their feet. Chicks hatch after 54 days of incubation, parents brood chicks for 30 to 35 days, then the chicks gather in crèches to wait out the Antarctic winter. In fact, chicks fast from May to August when their parents are foraging at sea. Beginning in September, parents return, regular feeding resumes, and chicks fledge from December through January at 10 to 13 months old. At the height of the Antarctic summer when food is plentiful, newly fledged chicks take to the sea. Adult birds molt before the next breeding and egg-laying begins.

When foraging at sea, king penguins may swim up to 30 km (20 mi.) from breeding beaches. Adults catch mainly small fish, diving as deep as 300 m (1,000 ft.). They may also feed on squid and shrimp. When feeding a chick, a parent bird may bring back as much as 3 kg (6.6 lb.) of food in its stomach.

Hunted for oil during the 1800s, king penguin populations declined, and some of their breeding islands remain empty. Today, most populations are increasing and recolonizing past breeding areas.

AT A GLANCE

SIZE: 94 cm (37 in.), 13.5 to 16 kg (30–35 lb.)

DISTRIBUTION: islands of the Southern Ocean, including the Falklands, South Georgia, Marion, Prince Edward, Crozet, Kerguelen, Heard and Macquarie.

POPULATION: about 1.6 million breeding pairs

CURRENT STATUS: not globally threatened

When someone mentions penguin, the image that most often comes to mind bears a striking resemblance to the Adélie (*Pygoscelis adeliae*)—the "typical" penguin. Totally black on its back and head and white on its belly, an Adélie's only decorative coloration is a white eye ring.

The name Adélie originated in 1840 during an Antarctic trip lead by the French explorer Captain Dumont d'Urville. While traveling, d'Urville named the area Terre Adelie, "Adélie Land" after his wife. Naturalists on the trip named the small black-and-white penguins on these islands Adélies.

Adélie penguins share the antarctic region with emperors but nest and raise chicks during the short summer season. Major colonies form in the Ross Sea region, on the Antarctic Peninsula and Scotia Arc, and around Prydz Bay. Cape Adare is home to the largest single colony exists with an estimated 282,000 breeding pairs.

Adélies begin returning to their previous season's nesting site in late October. Males usually arrive a few days before the females, establishing an area for a nest site. When females arrive, noisy courtship begins and pairs build nests of pebbles, bones, and moss.

After mating, females lay two eggs. Males incubate the eggs for the first 10 to 15 days while the females feed at sea. After 34 days eggs hatch and both parents brood chicks for 22 days. Chicks then gather in small crèches. Parents feed chicks once every day or two. Chicks fledge when 50 to 60 days old.

While on land, skuas (*Catharacta maccormicki*) prey on both eggs and chicks. At sea, leopard seals (*Hydrurga leptonyx*) hunt juveniles and adults. When foraging at the sea's surface, Adélies catch krill and young fish. Adélies do not need to dive deep (to 40 m or 131 ft.) but may swim far (up to 341 km or 211 mi.) from the colony.

AT A GLANCE

SIZE: 46 to 61 cm (18–24 in.), to 4.5 kg (10 lb.)

DISTRIBUTION: circumpolar on Antarctic continent within limits of pack-ice

POPULATION: 2.5 million breeding pairs worldwide current

STATUS: not globally threatened, stable or increasing

Gentoo Penguin

Orange-red bills and feet set these penguins apart from their close relatives, the Adélies and the chinstraps. Gentoos (*Pygoscelis papua*) also have a white "cap" extending from eye to eye over the top of their heads.

Rather timid and shy of people, "gentle" gentoos live around the islands of the Southern Ocean, breeding (in order of colony size) on the Falkland Islands, South Georgia, Kerguelen Island, the Antarctic Peninsula, and South Shetland Islands with smaller numbers on Heard, Macquarie, Staten, Orkney, and South Sandwich islands. About 108,000 pairs of birds nest at the largest site on Falkland Islands. Colonies are susceptible to human disturbance, and breeding numbers have decreased on Kerguelen Island where construction has recently occurred.

Some biologists split the gentoo population into two subspecies—one living around northern islands (*P.p. papua*) and another around the southern islands (*P.p. ellsworthii*)—due to differences in breeding biology. Generally, adults in the northern population stay near breeding grounds year-round, while those in the southern population leave nesting beaches from May to September.

In September, gentoos begin returning to the previous year's nesting site. Most birds reunite with former mates. Females lay two eggs between October and November. In northern populations, the breeding season is longer and females lay eggs as early as mid-June.

Eggs hatch in 34 to 36 days. Parents brood chicks for 25 to 35 days, taking turns protecting the nest and feeding at sea. When strong enough, chicks leave to form loose crèches, getting fed daily by parents. Chicks fledge and leave the colony after 80 to 100 days, usually in February.

After chicks leave, adults molt away from the nesting site, then spend most of their time at sea feeding on krill and fishes.

At a Glance

SIZE: 61 to 76 cm (24–30 in.), 5.5 to 6.4 kg (12–14 lb.)

DISTRIBUTION: circumpolar in subantactic and antarctic waters

POPULATION: 317,000 pairs

STATUS: not globally threatened

One of three species nick-named the "brush-tailed" penguins, chinstraps (*Pygoscelis antarctica*) have long, sleek tail feathers against which they often rest when on land. Chinstraps are aptly named, for they have a thin band of black feathers under the chin, stretching from ear to ear.

Chinstraps live in one of the coldest seas on Earth, the South Atlantic. They nest on subantarctic islands, usually establishing breeding colonies on South Shetland, South Orkney, South Sandwich, South Georgia, and Bouvet. They also nest along the shoreline of the Antarctic Peninsula but not along the mainland coast.

Chinstrap populations are steady or growing. The South Sandwich Islands have the largest population of nesting chinstraps, an estimated 5 million pairs.

Breeding begins in September, when adult birds return to ice-free beaches and establish territories. Most birds return to the same nesting site as the previous year, and pair up with previous mates. Partners build round, shallow nests of small stones, often adding bones, feathers, or other small items found on the beach.

Females lay two eggs, usually during November or December, and both parents incubate eggs for about 33 to 35 days. Chicks hatch in December or January. Parents brood and guard chicks in shifts of 12 to 24 hours. While one parent broods, the other feeds at sea, and brings back food. After 20 to 30 days, chicks leave their nests and gather with other chicks in crèches. Parents continue to feed chicks until late February or March when chicks reach 50 to 60 days old.

After chicks leave, adults molt in March and April. They spend the remaining months at sea, feeding and regaining weight lost during breeding and molting. Chinstraps eat mostly crustaceans, such as krill and amphipods, and some-times small fishes.

AT A GLANCE

SIZE: 46 to 61 cm (18–24 in.), 4 kg (9 lb.)

DISTRIBUTION: antarctic and subantarctic islands

POPULATION: about 7.5 million pairs

current status: not globally threatened

Rockhopper Penguin

The rockhopper penguin (*Eudyptes chrysocome*) has a bounce in its step. When on land the rockhopper doesn't always walk; it sometimes hops, jumping from rock to rock while holding its wings and tail outstretched.

Rockhoppers live on many islands of the Southern Ocean. Scientists have noticed slight differences in size and coloration and have designated three subspecies. *E.c. chrysocome* has short, golden head feathers and breeds only on islands close to Cape Horn and the Falkland Islands. *E.c. filholi* breeds on Marion, Crozet, Kerguelen, Heard, Macquarie, and Campbell islands. *E.c. moseleyi* has the longest head feathers of the three subspecies and breeds on the more northern islands of the Tristan de Cunha group, Amsterdam, and St. Paul islands.

Generally, nesting sites are on beaches with easy access to the sea although these penguins are able to navigate rocky shorelines too. Adults return to nesting sites in October through November, with pairs making shallow depressions in the ground for nests. Some penguins may add stones, sticks, or clumps of moss. Females lay two eggs. The first egg is significantly smaller, and is often lost.

The second egg incubates for 32 to 34 days. After each parent takes a short two-day shift, the female stays on the nest for 12 days by herself, and then the male incubates the egg another 14 days. The female returns a couple of days before the chick hatches. Chicks remain in the nest for about 24 to 26 days. The males stay with the chick during the day, guarding the nest while the female goes to sea, feeds, and returns to feed the chick. When strong enough, the chicks gather in crèches. Females continue to feed young while males feed themselves after their fast. Then both parents feed chicks until they fledge at 65 to 75 days.

Rockhoppers generally eat krill, amphipods, and small fishes.

AT A GLANCE

SIZE: 41 to 46 cm (16-18 in.), about 2.3 to 2.7 kg (5-6 lb.)

DISTRIBUTION: subantarctic islands

POPULATION: about 1.8 million breeding pairs

CURRENT STATUS: IUCN category: *Vulnerable*; Extinction of some localized breeding populations of subspecies is possible.

One of the most numerous of all penguins, macaronis (*Eudyptes chrysolophus*) live among the many islands of the Southern Ocean including the Falklands, South Georgia, South Sandwich, South Orkneys, South Shetlands, Bouvet, Prince Edward, Marion, Crozet, Kerguelen, and Heard islands along with some areas of the Antarctic Peninsula and southern Chile. The number of breeding pairs on South Georgia Island alone numbers 2.7 million pairs.

As a crested penguin, macaronis have the characteristic long, golden head feathers. To early explorers, these head feathers resembled a fashionable hairstyle worn by "Macaroni Club" members in London. Men with this hairstyle were called "mac-aronis," hence explorers named these lively, feathered penguins with fancy "hair" macaronis.

The breeding season begins in late October and early November as adults begin returning to previous years' nesting sites. Last year's mates often find each other again. Females lay two eggs in November; the first egg is usually one third smaller than the second egg and rarely hatches.

Males and females incubate the larger eggs for 33 to 37 days, trading places in three long shifts. The male guards and broods the chick after hatching, the female makes trips from the nest to the ocean to feed the chick. Chicks form crèches when 23 to 25 days old and fledge at 60 to 70 days. After chicks leave, adults feed at sea, then molt at or near breeding sites. The remaining time before the next breeding season is spent at sea.

Macaronis eat krill, usually diving between 15 to 50 m (49–164 ft.), and staying under water for one to two minutes. When raising chicks, most birds go to sea during the day, leaving the colony in the early morning and returning each evening. As chicks grow older, foraging trips may be longer, possibly a day to a day and a half.

AT A GLANCE

SIZE: 51 to 61 cm (20–24 in.), 4.5 kg (10 lb.)

DISTRIBUTION: subantarctic islands in the Atlantic and Indian oceans

POPULATION: about 9 million breeding pairs

CURRENT STATUS: not globally threatened, but some populations in danger; IUCN category: *Near Threatened*.

One of the largest of the crested penguins, the royal (*Eudyptes schlegeli*), lives around Macquarie Island and sometimes appears along southern coasts of New Zealand and Australia. Its long, orange-yellow and black head feathers start at the top of the bill and fall back over the head to droop behind the eye.

Royals breed only on Macquarie Island, where scientists have counted 57 colonies ranging in size from 75,000 to 160,000 breeding pairs. Adults return to previous year's nesting areas in late September after spending the winter foraging at sea. Pairs nest on open, sandy, or rocky grounds without vegetation but with small pebbles.

After mating and courtship, females lay two eggs. Similar to other crested penguins, the first egg is much smaller than the second egg (about 63 percent of the size). The first egg is often lost. If the smaller chick does hatch, it often cannot successfully compete with the larger chick and perishes.

Both parents incubate the egg(s) for 35 days, alternating nest duties with feeding at sea. The male broods the chick for the first 10 to 12 days, then is relieved by the female. Most chicks leave the nest after three weeks to gather together in crèches. Both parents take turns feeding chicks every two to three days. Chicks begin to fledge when 65 days old and leave the nesting area. Adults then return to sea to feed. After about a month, they are back on land to molt at the now vacant breeding sites.

Because these birds breed only on Macquarie Island and do not range far from shore, the threat of harm from habitat destruction (natural or human caused) is great.

Although not well documented, scientists believe royals eat krill, small fishes, and cephalopods depending on the time of year and location of foraging area.

AT A GLANCE

SIZE: 66 to 76 cm (26-30 in.), 5.5 kg (12 lb.)

DISTRIBUTION: Macquarie and Campbell Islands; also around the New Zealand coast

POPULATION: 850,000 breeding pairs

CURRENT STATUS: IUCN category: *Vulnerable*

Photo by Tui de Roy, Minden Pictures.

Resembling their close relatives the Snares Island penguins, Fiordland crested penguins (*Eudyptes pachyrhynchus*) live around New Zealand and southern Australia, breeding on the west and southwest coasts of South Island (New Zealand), and nearby islands like Stewart.

Difficult to tell apart when wet and at sea, the Snares Island and Fiordland crested are easier to distinguish when on land. Fiordland crested penguins have small white streaks on their cheeks and very little exposed skin around the base of their heavier, darker bill.

Fiordland crested penguins nest among the dense vegetation of shoreline temperate rainforests. They may burrow or hide among shrubs and vines, or in ground cover of ferns and mosses. On rocky coasts, they may nest among fallen rocks, in caves, or under overhangs.

Breeding season begins in June with adults returning from winter feeding grounds. Most mates pair again and build nests away from other nests. Females lay two eggs of almost equal size. Both parents incubate eggs and brood chicks.

One study at a colony at Jackson Head showed only half of the parents raising one chick to fledging age. Natural hazards took the heaviest toll. Heavy rainfall washed chicks out of the nest, and in some areas, wekas (*Gallirallus australis*) took many chicks.

Chicks fledge and go to sea at about 75 days of age. Then parents feed at sea for 60 to 80 days, eating squids, krill and fishes, before returning to the nesting beach to molt.

The IUCN lists Fiordland crested penguins as vulnerable. Accurate population counts are difficult because of this bird's nesting habits. Some breeding sites cannot be reached and nests are often well camouflaged among dense vegetation. Even so, some regional populations have declined as much as 30 percent in the past 10 years.

AT A GLANCE

SIZE: 61 cm (24 in.), 2.5 to 3.0 kg (5.5–6.6 lb.)

DISTRIBUTION: subantarctic islands and New Zealand

POPULATION: 2,500 to 3,000 nests (possibly 10,000 birds)

CURRENT STATUS: IUCN category: *Vulnerable*; CITES: not listed

Photo by Tui de Roy, Minden Pictures.

Erect-crested Penguin

With perky head crests that tilt upward off the back of the head, erect-crested penguins (*Eudyptes sclateri*) often have a surprised look. These medium-sized penguins live only on and around New Zealand, breeding on Antipodes and Bounty islands. Their heads and backs are black with white chests and bellies. Their orangish-brown bills are more slender than those of other crested penguins.

Only a few scientists have studied the breeding behavior of erect-crested penguins; many details are still unknown. The breeding season begins in early September when adults return from winter feeding. Pairs build simple nests, a shallow depression on flat ground or between large boulders. Penguins rim the circle with stones, sometimes adding grass. Rookeries are dense with nests crowded close together. Females lay two eggs, the first barely half the size of the second (55 percent). Incubation of eggs and brooding of chicks are probably similar to other crested penguin species: both parents incubate eggs, usually the first egg or chick is lost, brooding duties are shared, and the chick fledges at about 70 days old. Scientists don't know if mating pairs reunite each season, or if adults use the previous year's nesting site. Adults probably molt after chicks leave rookeries. Adults spend winter months away from breeding sites.

IUCN classifies erect-crested penguins as endangered. During the past 20 years, the penguin population on Antipodes Island has declined 50 percent and completely disappeared from past nesting sites on Campbell Island. Population stability on Bounty Island is unknown. No single cause for these declines has been identified but they are probably due to changes in food availability, ocean conditions, and nesting habitats along with increased human interactions.

At a Glance

SIZE: 64 cm (25 in.), 2.5 to 3.5 kg (5.5-7.7 lb.)

DISTRIBUTION: Australia; New Zealand; and Bounty, Campbell, and Auckland islands

POPULATION: 165,000-175,000 breeding pairs

CURRENT STATUS: IUCN category: *Endangered*; CITES: not listed

Snares Island Penguin

Named after their only breeding location, Snares Island penguins (*Eudyptes robustus*) range among the islands and coastlines of New Zealand up to Tasmania and the southern tip of Australia. Their territory overlaps that of other crested penguins: the macaroni, erect-crested, and Fiordland crested penguins.

Although similar in appearance to other crested penguins, Snares Island penguins have a unique strip of bare pinkish-white skin along the base of the bill.

Snares Island penguins nest along the coast in flat, muddy areas, or on gently sloping rocks among small trees or thickets. Adults return to breeding sites in late August and early September, creating closely packed colonies. Females lay two eggs sometime from mid-September to mid-October. The first egg is usually smaller than the second. Both parents incubate eggs (31 to 37 days), and chicks hatch while the male is on the nest. Males continue to brood chicks for three weeks while females make feeding trips to and from the sea. After three weeks, chicks leave the nest to join crèches until they fledge at about 75 days old. Usually parents raise only the chick from the second-laid egg. First chicks are often taken by predators or die from lack of food due to competition from the second, stronger chick. Adults molt at the breeding site after feeding at sea for two months or more.

Although not well studied, the feeding behavior of Snares Island penguins is probably similar to other crested penguin species living in the area. During the breeding season, they feed primarily on krill, foraging during the day and returning to the colony at night.

Although populations are believed to be stable, IUCN lists Snares Island penguins as vulnerable. The species' limited range and very small, specific breeding area puts them at risk during adverse weather or large oil spills.

AT A GLANCE

SIZE: 63.5 cm (25 in.), to 3.0 kg (6.6 lb.)

DISTRIBUTION: restricted to Snares Island, south of New Zealand

POPULATION: 23,250 breeding pairs

CURRENT STATUS: IUCN category: *Vulnerable*; CITES: not listed

Photo by Tui de Roy, Minden Pictures.

Yellow-eyed Penguin

This striking penguin (*Megadyptes antipodes*) has many unique characteristics: it's the third largest penguin, it's the only member in the penguin family Megadyptes, its nesting behavior is the least colonial of any penguin species, and it's the only penguin with yellow eyes and head feathers.

Yellow-eyed penguins live only around southern New Zealand and the nearby islands like Auckland and Campbell. Adults stay within the breeding area year-round and nest in secluded areas away from other yellow-eyed penguin nests. Nesting sites are often covered with native flax and lupine plants. Yellow-eyed penguins prefer small bays or the headlands of large bays, making nests on the shore, sea-facing slopes, gullies, and cliff-tops.

The breeding season begins in September with previous year's mates pairing again. Females lay two equal-sized eggs sometime during September or October. Both parents incubate their eggs, usually changing places at the nest every couple of days. After 39 to 51 days, eggs hatch, and chicks stay in the nest for the next 40 to 50 days. Parents take turns brooding and guarding chicks. Chicks do not form crèches but stay close to the nest. They fledge after 106 to 108 days. Adults usually begin molting three weeks after chicks have fledged. More than half of the nesting adults raise both chicks to fledging (estimate of 60 percent). While predators carry off and eat many chicks, human activity also often disturbs nest sites.

Yellow-eyed penguins eat mostly small fishes like opalfish (*Hemerocoetes monopterygius*), red cod (*Pseudophycis bachus*), sprats (*Sprattus antipodum*), and blue cod (*Parapercis colias*). Some also take squids. Most forage daily, leaving the nest site or shoreline at sunrise and returning in the evening. Feeding dives are not deep, most prey is caught from the surface to 34 m (111.5 ft.).

AT A GLANCE

SIZE: size: 76 cm (30 in.), 6 kg (13 lb.)

DISTRIBUTION: southeast New Zealand

POPULATION: between 5,100 and 6,200 individuals

CURRENT STATUS: IUCN category: *Vulnerable*; CITES: not listed. Considered rare on Campbell, Auckland, and Stewart Islands.

62

Photo by Konrad Wothe, Minden Pictures.

The smallest of all penguins, the fairy or little blue penguins (*Eudyptula minor*) stand only 35 cm (14 in.) tall. These shy birds live along the coasts of New Zealand, southern Australia, and the nearby islands. They spend the day feeding at sea, coming ashore in the evening to rest at night.

Within their range, fairy penguins show differences in appearance. In general, southern fairy penguins are darker and more steely blue than the northern individuals. In addition, the northern individuals have extra white color on the leading and trailing edges of their flippers. The differences in color and the isolated breeding areas of these individuals has led some scientists to suggest the northern group is separate, calling them the white-flippered penguin (*Eudyptula albosignata*).

Fairy penguins have breeding colonies at many points along the south coast of Australia, around Tasmania, and on the coast of New Zealand. Adults live close to breeding areas year-round and rarely mix with other colonies at other locations. With little cross breeding between colonies, slight differences have appeared specific to certain areas. Some scientists have suggested six subspecies for fairy penguins, *E.m. albosignata*, *E.m. novaehollandiae*, *E.m. iredalei*, *E.m. variabilis*, *E.m. minor* and *E.m. chathamensis*.

Across the breeding range, mating pairs may begin courtship anywhere from June to October. Breeding pairs burrow into the ground, lining nests with surrounding vegetation. Depending on soil conditions, pairs may take several weeks to prepare their nests. In areas without soil, birds nest under rocks, in caves or crevices, or under bushes. Females lay two equal-sized eggs. Incubation lasts about 33 to 39 days. Parents brood chicks for 7 to 10 days and guard for another 13 to 20 days. Chicks fledge when 50 to 65 days old. Adults molt soon afterward.

AT A GLANCE

SIZE: 41 cm (16 in.), about 1.0 kg (2.2 lb.)

DISTRIBUTION: southern Australia and New Zealand

POPULATION: between 700,000 and 1,200,000 individuals

CURRENT STATUS: not globally threatened

Photo by Fred Bavendam, Minden Pictures.

Magellanic penguins (*Spheniscus magellanicus*) inhabit the coastline and off-shore islands of southern South America including the Falkland Islands. They adapt to a wide range of temperature conditions, from nesting on the hot beaches of Argentina to feeding in the cold offshore waters rich with fishes.

Similar in appearance to African, Humboldt, and Galápagos penguins, Magellanics have bare patches of pink skin around the eye and base of the bill. Magellanics are distinguished from other *Spheniscus* penguins by having not one but two black bands across the chest.

Magellanics spend non-breeding months (May through August) at sea feeding. Birds return to breeding rookeries, and usually to the previous year's nest site, in September or October. Mates meet at the nest site and often pair for another breeding season.

Pairs may dig or re-inhabit previous year's burrow nests which may be as long as 1 m (3 ft.) with a circular nesting chamber at the end. Nests may also be made under bushes or in the open.

Females lay two eggs of similar size with both parents sharing incubation duties. Eggs hatch in about 39 to 42 days. Parents guard chicks for another 29 days, then leave chicks unattended while collecting food at sea. At this stage, parents feed chicks every one to three days. At 60 to 70 days, chicks fledge and leave to fend for themselves at sea. Adults molt after the chicks go to sea.

Adults catch mainly anchovies and sardines with occasional squids and crustaceans although changes in diet items depend on time of year and location of feeding. While raising chicks, parents feed close to the rookery. After molting, adults disperse at sea from May to August, often traveling north to follow anchovy populations along the coasts of Peru and Brazil.

AT A GLANCE

SIZE: 61 to 71 cm (24-28 in.), 5 kg (11 lb.)

DISTRIBUTION: Falkland Islands and along the coasts of Chile and Argentina

POPULATION: about 1.3 million pairs

CURRENT STATUS: some populations near threatened; IUCN category: *Lower Risk*

Named after the cold-water current off the coast of South America, Humboldt penguins (*Spheniscus humboldti*) are the only penguins living along the arid coastlines of northern Chile and Peru. Like other warm-weather *Spheniscus* penguins, Humboldts have bare patches of pink skin around the base of their bills and eyes.

With the southern range of Humboldts slightly over-lapping the northern range of Magellanics, bird watchers may confuse the identity of these two birds. The penguins' body coloration is similar but the two can be distinguished by black chest stripes—Humboldts have one, while Magellanics have two.

Humboldt penguins remain near breeding areas year-round. Ongoing studies in Peru and Chile have documented two main egg-laying periods, from October to November and another from April to May. Biologists observing Humboldts at zoos have noted females usually lay two eggs with both parents incubating the eggs for about 40 days.

Humboldts are an endangered species. Populations have declined significantly since the mid-1800s when local industries began excavating guano (bird excrement) from offshore islands. Guano is then sold as fertilizer to the United States and Europe. Humboldts dig burrows into the soft guano, which in some places is 20 m (66 ft.) deep. Without this substrate, Humboldts cannot dig burrows, and lose all chicks.

Changes in ocean temperature also affect Humboldt populations. The cold-water Humboldt current is sometimes displaced when changes in atmospheric wind patterns push warm water across the Pacific Ocean to the coastlines of South America. Anchovies and sar-dines, the main food fish for Humboldts, move away with the colder water. During these El Niño events, most chicks and many adults die of starvation.

AT A GLANCE

SIZE: 56 to 66 cm (22–26 in.), 4 kg (9 lb.)

DISTRIBUTION: coastlines of Chile and Peru, islands off the west coast of South America

POPULATION: about 33,000 birds

CURRENT STATUS: IUCN category: *Vulnerable*; CITES: *Appendix I* Peruvian government considers these birds in danger of extinction.

African Penguin

African penguins (*Spheniscus demersus*) have also been called black-footed or jackass (after their loud donkeylike braying) penguins. They are the only penguins living on the African continent, ranging from Namibia on the west coast, around the Cape of Good Hope to Algoa Bay, South Africa. Nesting colonies are widespread throughout this area, making accurate population estimates difficult.

Like other warm-weather penguins, Africans have bare patches of skin around their eyes and at the base of their bill. These featherless areas help dissipate excess body heat when penguins become too warm.

Africans nest along coastlines, making burrows in soft soil when possible. If the nesting area doesn't have appropriate soil, birds build nests under bushes or boulders. Adults stay within breeding areas year round. Nests are semi-colonial, not close together like macaronis but not as far apart as yellow-eyed penguins.

Females may lay eggs at any time of the year but, depending on the location, egg-laying peaks occur from February to May and November to December. Females usually lay two eggs, the first being larger than the second. Both parents incubate eggs in one- to two-day shifts for about 38 to 41 days. After hatching, chicks are brooded for up to 40 days. Chicks remain in or near the nest until fledging, anywhere between 70 and 100 days old. Adults may molt before they begin breeding or after the chicks have fledged.

African penguins primarily eat anchovies (*Engraulis capensis*) but also may eat squids and krill. They usually feed during the day, catching most prey above 30 m (98 ft.).

South Africa considers the African penguin an endangered species, citing vulnerability of nesting habitat to damage by oil spills, guano harvesting, and pollution, in addition to the threat of over fishing foraging areas.

AT A GLANCE

SIZE: 61 to 71 cm (24-28 in.), 3.0 kg (6.6 lb.)

DISTRIBUTION: South African waters

POPULATION: 56,000 breeding pairs

CURRENT STATUS: IUCN category: *Vulnerable*; CITES: *Appendix II* general decline continues, Endangered on U.S. Endangered Species List

S itting on the equator, the Galápagos Islands play host to a number of unusual animals. So it's not surprising to find a penguin living here in the tropics.

The smallest of the warm-weather penguins, Galápagos penguins (*Spheniscus mendiculus*) stand just 45 cm (18 in.). They have gray-black heads, cheeks, and chins, and one black band across their white chests. While most penguins must contend with ice and snow, Galápagos penguins must keep cool to survive. One way Galápagos penguins lose body heat is through bare patches of skin at the base of the bill. Their small size also increases the body surface to mass ratio, resulting in a bigger proportion of outside body surface in contact with air or water.

Galápagos penguins primarily breed on two islands, Fernandina and Isabela. Adults stay near breeding grounds and pairs may nest at any time during the year. Females lay two eggs of similar size. Parents incubate eggs for 38 to 40 days. After hatching, parents share brooding duties until chicks fledge at 60 to 65 days old. Adults molt after chicks go to sea.

The successful raising of chicks depends on many factors. If sea temperatures rise (such as in El Niño years), food becomes scarce and chicks die of starvation. In addition, land predators such as native snakes and introduced rats, feral dogs, and cats take eggs and chicks. Currently, population numbers are down and these penguins are considered endangered. A large El Niño event in 1982 to 1983 resulted in more than 70 percent of the entire penguin colony dying, with numbers dropping to an estimated 500 individuals. During the next 15 years, the population fluctuated as "good" El Niño summers followed "bad" summers with reduced food supplies. Today the population is estimated at more than 1,000 but the numbers are still not as high as the early 1980s.

AT A GLANCE

SIZE: 53 cm (21 in.), 2.5 kg (5.5 lb.)

DISTRIBUTION: Galápagos Islands, on the equator off the coast of Ecuador.

POPULATION: estimated at 1,200 to 1,500 individuals

CURRENT STATUS: IUCN category: *Endangered*; CITES not listed

---

Photo by Tui de Roy, Minden Pictures.

Penguins in Peril

"*I have often had the impression that to penguins, man is just another penguin— different, less predictable, occasionally violent, but tolerable company when he sits still and minds his own business.*"

Bernard Stonehouse

Gentoo penguin
and fur seal (*Arctocephalus australis*)

The lifestyles of penguins cause risky situations on many levels. To reproduce, penguins need undisturbed coastal areas free of land predators. These areas need to remain consistent from year to year, as penguins return to previous year's nesting sites. Penguin prey—krill, small fishes, and squids—live in clean, nutrient-rich, cold-water currents upwelling along the coast. Penguins need prey close to shore, as most forage short distances when feeding chicks. In today's world of ever increasing human population, these delicate coastal habitats are prime targets for development and offer little resistance to environmental exploitation.

 *Natural Threats*

In the past, natural threats posed the biggest danger to penguin survival.

Weather. Long-term or drastic climate changes pose the greatest threat to penguins. Changes in sea-ice formation, ocean currents, wind patterns, and storm cycles affect penguin survival rates. Around Antarctica, many penguin species follow the ice edge as it forms during the winter and retreats during the summer. The availability and abundance of food and appropriate nesting sites is linked to this movement. Along the coastline of western South America, Humboldt penguin populations decline during El Niño years when ocean surface temperatures warm significantly. In

1982–1983, a severe El Niño event occurred, reducing the overall seabird population along the coast from 6 million birds to 300,000. A similar event occurred at Campbell Island where 1.7 million rockhopper penguins nested in the 1940s. When water temperature rose and food became scarce, rockhopper populations fell to 105,000 by the early 1990s. A very real threat to the Galápagos penguins is the possible movement of the cold-water Cromwell Current that flows around the islands. If it were to disappear or decrease its flow, Galápagos penguins probably would not survive.

Early or late seasonal storms, either snow or rainfall, can disrupt breeding activities. Chicks may freeze or get swept to sea. Adults may leave nests unattended to seek shelter at sea, leaving young chicks to fend for themselves.

Ocean predators. Leopard seals, fur seals, and sea lions often prey on penguins. Leopard seals inhabit the coastlines of Antarctica and catch penguins at sea, at the edges of sea-ice, and along shores where penguins are leaving and returning from breeding sites. Subantarctic fur seals catch penguins at sea and sometimes share beaches with breeding penguins. Penguins can get caught between fighting males or be attacked. To a lesser extent, killer whales and sharks attack and sometimes eat penguins.

Land predators. In the Antarctic and Subantarctic, the skua (a gull-like bird) takes the most chicks and eggs. Skuas may work in pairs to obtain their prey. One bird distracts the penguin on the nest, and the other swoops in to steal the egg or chick. Skuas also take chicks that have strayed from the protection of the nest or crèche or are

Hungry leopard seals prey on Adélie penguins. Adélies often escape capture by jumping on nearby ice floes.

sickly and too weak to defend themselves. Sheathbills and giant petrels may prey on chicks and take eggs. Sheathbills also intercept chinstrap regurgitation as penguin parents feed their offspring. In higher, warmer latitudes, gulls and ibises eat penguin eggs. Large southern elephant seals beached next to penguin colonies may crush penguin eggs, chicks, and adults as they move along the beach.

Direct Human Impact

As European explorers traveled south and began harvesting penguins, whales, and fish, the impact of human activity on animal populations grew quickly.

Hunting and egging. Sailors, hunters, and explorers killed penguins for their meat, fat, feathers, and skin in addition to taking eggs from nests. For example, during 1897 records show more than 700,000 eggs taken from the African penguin rookeries along the coast of South Africa. Today scientists estimate the total population at 180,500. The production of penguin oil during the late 1800s and early 1900s destroyed some penguin colonies. One company in the Falkland Islands reported taking 405,000 penguins for their oil in 1867. Modern day fishermen from Chile and Peru still hunt Humboldt penguins, killing the birds to reduce competition for anchovies, sardines, and other fish.

Urban coastal development. Today, the human impact on penguin populations is less direct but just as damaging. Coastlines are popular places for both penguins and people. Housing, agriculture, ranching, shipping, logging, and mining destroy habitats where penguins usually nest. The yellow-eyed penguins of New Zealand have lost most of their forested nesting habitat to land clearing. Guano (dried bird excrement) mining on the offshore islands of Chile and South Africa has severely affected the populations of African and Humboldt penguins. Without the soft layer of guano in which to dig, these birds nest in dangerous, unprotected areas, which leads to high chick mortality.

Pollution. Marine pollution tends to concentrate in coastal and sur-face waters, two places where penguins frequently swim. Oil spills pose the biggest danger, not only from the initial release but also from long-term degradation of offshore water that may change prey distribution. Other pollutants such as pesticides, heavy metals, and plastics reach coastal waters through river systems or are dumped off-shore. These may not directly kill penguins, but chemicals can concentrate in food fish and affect breeding success rates or fishing and plastic debris can entangle individuals.

This gentoo penguin became entangled in a discarded net and stranded on a beach in the Falkland Islands.
Photo by Frans Lanting, Minden Pictures.

Over fishing. Increased interest in fish stocks living in the Southern Ocean has caused speculation on how more commercial fishing will affect penguin populations. Over-harvesting of penguin prey species (fishes, squids, krill) may cause a decline in populations. As prey populations decline, competition between fisheries and penguins (in addition to other animals) increases.

Exotic species. Another threat comes from introduced species like stoats, ferrets, rats, and feral cats and dogs. In addition to preying on penguins, exotic species carry disease, either directly or through ticks, lice, and fleas. Avian malaria, Newcastle disease virus, and fowl pox virus spread this way and can kill both adults and chicks. The establishment of settlements in remote areas and increasing worldwide travel continually pose dangers of introducing harmful species and diseases.

 *Conservation Efforts*

Currently all 17 species of penguins are legally protected under various laws and regulations. At least five species are considered at risk of extinction: the Humboldt, the Galápagos, the erect-crested, yellow-eyed, and African penguins.

Penguins living everywhere come under The Convention on International Trade in Endangered Species of Wild Fauna and Flora

Cleaned and nourished, African penguins recover in an enclosed pen before being released to the ocean.

Deadly Oil Spill

On June 23, 2000, ore carrier Treasure sank near Cape Town, South Africa, leaking 1,250 tons of fuel oil into the surrounding water. The ship went down between Dassen and Robben Islands, two prime breeding areas for African penguins. Dassen Island supports the largest breeding colony while Robben Island holds the third largest colony.

Responding to the challenge, the Southern African National Foundation for the Conservation of Coastal Birds (SANCCOB) organized dozens of other organizations and 40,000 volunteers to coordinate one of the largest and most successful bird rescue efforts ever. As the call for volunteers went out, SeaWorld responded by sending two staff members who helped organize flights and coordinate efforts with personnel in South Africa.

For six weeks, crews worked 15-hour days, collecting, washing, drying, feeding, and caring for oiled birds. SANCCOB based the cleanup effort at Salt River Station, a large railroad car maintenance building in Cape Town, South Africa. Here volunteers placed collected birds in shallow, dry pools about 3 m (10 ft.) in diameter and constructed of wire with a vinyl liner. About 80 birds stayed in each pool with 40 to 60 pools to a room. Trained staff assessed newly arrived penguins, giving fluids, extra iron supplements, and other medical treatment where needed. Volunteers bathed penguins by first coating them with vegetable oil to dissolve the tanker oil, then washing them with dishwashing soap. After a rinsing with fresh water, penguins sat under warm heat lamps overnight to dry.

Clean birds also received fluids, vitamins, iron supplement, and a flipper band for identification. On a good day, volunteers cleaned 500 to 600 penguins. The last bird rescued received its bath on August 6, 2000.

In the end, the effort collected and cleaned about 22,000 oiled penguins, of which 90 percent survived. Volunteers saved an additional 21,000 penguins by collecting unoiled penguins, trucking them to Port Elizabeth, and releasing them to swim home. Most of these individuals arrived home after the worst stage of the oil spill was over.

(CITES), an international treaty developed in 1973 to regulate trade in certain wildlife species. CITES categorizes various animals according to their current status. Appendix I lists species identified as currently endangered, or in danger of extinction. Appendix II lists species as threatened, or likely to become endangered. Appendix III lists species needing additional protection, but are not yet considered endangered or threatened.

Penguins living in Antarctica are additionally protected by the Antarctic Treaty, signed by 12 nations in 1959 and reauthorized in 1991. The Treaty makes it illegal to harm, or in any way interfere with, a penguin or its eggs. Every penguin specimen collected with a permit must be approved by and reported to the Scientific Committee for Antarctic Research (SCAR).

Another program that helps penguins is the Conservation Assessment and Management Plan (CAMP), an assessment tool to evaluate the status of various animals and to determine conservation priorities. The Captive Breeding Specialist Group (CBSG) of the Species Survival Commission of the International Union for the Conservation of Nature and Natural Resources (IUCN)/World Conservation Union developed CAMP.

Many places in the world have established wildlife refuges, some as early as the early 1900s. In 1919 the Tasmanian government stopped all exploitation of penguins on Macquarie Island and proclaimed the island a sanctuary. In 1924 the French declared the Kerguelen Islands off Antarctica a National Park.

Worldwide conferences for penguin specialists help keep information current and solutions to problems focused. The Fourth International Penguin Conference brought nearly 100 researchers and conservationists together at La Serena/Coquimbo, Chile in September, 2000. With more than 50 presentations, topics ranged from up-to-date census of species like the Humboldt to cutting-edge research with the latest methods and instruments such as smaller and more powerful telemetry devices for tracking penguin movements. Recommendations were made for the direction of further research both in the field and with captive breeding programs.

Zoological parks continue to play an important role in penguin conservation. Most people do not have the opportunity to observe penguins in the wild. The unique ability to observe and learn directly from live animals increases public awareness and appreciation of wildlife.

Currently the three SeaWorld parks maintain emperor, king, Adélie, gentoo, chinstrap, rockhopper, macaroni, Magellanic, and Humboldt penguins. Each of these species has successfully reproduced within the parks' comprehensive breeding program.

In 1980, SeaWorld San Diego became the only park to successfully breed emperor penguins outside the Antarctic. That year, three emperor pairs raised chicks. Two years later, "E.P." hatched and became the first emperor penguin to be hand raised. Overall, 19 emperor chicks have hatched at SeaWorld San Diego's facility.

In addition to emperors, SeaWorld's penguin breeding successes include the first macaroni chick to be conceived and hatched at SeaWorld in 1990, and the first chinstrap penguin to hatch outside the Antarctic in 1991.

SeaWorld participates in a worldwide captive propagation and

Aviculturists at SeaWorld San Diego help care for emperor penguins. Overall 19 emperor chicks have hatched since 1980.

management program for threatened or endangered species in the wild. SeaWorld San Diego participates the Species Survival Plan for the endangered Humboldt penguin. SeaWorld's colony has become the most successful in the program with more than 100 chicks hatched and raised since the 1970s. Aviculture staff have also traveled to Humboldt colonies to help conduct population counts and monitor guano harvesting.

SeaWorld staff participate in yearly Galápagos penguin counts through the Charles Darwin Research Station on the Galápagos Islands, Ecuador. The project lays the foundation for regular counts of the penguins. This allows scientists to estimate population size, distribution and abundance, nesting locations and nesting success.

In addition, SeaWorld parks also employ two studbook keepers to

Dr. Ann Bowles, Hubbs-SeaWorld Research Institute scientist, recorded the vocalizations of emperor penguins. Dr. Bowles determined each bird had an individually distinctive call.

track the captive breeding of chinstrap and king penguins.

A penguin's future is in our hands. Looking into the future health of penguin populations is a risky business. Many factors affect the continued stability of most penguin species and the uncertain survival of the five endangered species—the Humboldt, the Galápagos, the erect-crested, yellow-eyed, and African. With an ever-increasing human population comes the push for more and more living space and food. And reversing the threats of coastal development, habitat degradation, and over fishing is difficult at best. Promoting and supporting penguin research projects, breeding programs, and education programs or even spreading the word about penguins helps. Continued success depends on everyone's involvement, no matter how small.

adaptation—a modification that makes an animal better suited for its environment.

Antarctic—the continent of Antarctica or the region surrounding it.

Aves—scientific class containing all birds; warm-blooded animals with feathers.

CITES—The Convention on International Trade in Endangered Species of Wild Fauna and Flora. Treaty signed in 1973 to regulate international trade for certain species.

clutch—a nest of eggs.

countershading—a type of camouflage in which the coloration of the dorsal (back) side of an animal is darker than the ventral (belly) side of an animal.

endangered—may become extinct by human-made or natural changes in the environment.

environment—the total surroundings and forces that act upon a living thing.

equator—the imaginary circle around the center of the Earth, equal distance at all points from the North and South Pole.

down—the fine, soft feathers of a chick (baby bird); also the soft underfeathers of adult birds.

fledge—to acquire the feathers necessary for flight.

flipper—a broad, flat limb containing bones and modified for swimming.

food chain—a straight-line diagram that shows "who eats whom" in an ecosystem.

food web—a diagram that shows the complex interconnections of "who eats whom" in an ecosystem.

forage—to search for food.

habitat—the place where an animal lives.

ice floe—a flat expanse of floating ice.

IUCN—International Union for the Conservation of Nature and Natural Resources. This conservation organization's goal is to provide leadership and promote a worldwide approach to conservation. In 1993, its membership included 655 organizations representing 103 countries.

krill—a shrimplike crustacean in the family Euphausiidae.

metabolism—biochemical processes by which animals generate energy.

molt—*v.* to shed old feathers and grow new ones.

petrel—antarctic seabird that preys on penguin chicks and eggs.

pip—*v.* to break through the shell of an egg.

predator—an animal that eats other animals. An introduced predator is a predator that doesn't naturally occur in an animal's environment but was brought there by people.

preen—clean, rearrange, and oil feathers.

prey—*v*: to hunt and eat other animals. *n*: an animal eaten by another animal.

rookery—the nesting location of a large group of birds.

sheathbill—a white antarctic shorebird that preys on penguin chicks and eggs.

skua—a gull-like anatarctic seabird that preys on penguin chicks and eggs.

Species Survival Plan— a program for managing captive populations of certain threatened or endangered animals, administered by the American Zoo and Aquarium Association (AZA).

studbook—a comprehensive record of all births, deaths, and inter-institutional transfers of a particular species.

threatened—facing a possible threat of extinction, but not facing as great a threat as an endangered species. Threatened species are likely to become endangered.

weka—a flightless bird native to New Zealand. Wekas may prey on penguin chicks. Wekas are also called woodhens.

Bibliography

Ashworth, William. *Penguins, Puffins, and Auks. Their Lives and Behavior.* New York: Crown Publishers, Inc., 1993.

Conservation Breeding Specialist Group. *Penguin Conservation Assessment and Management Plan.* Proceedings from September 8–9, 1996 workshop held in Cape Town, South Africa. Minneapolis, Minnesota: 1998.

Croxall, J.P. and L.S. Davis. "Penguins: Paradoxes and Patterns." *Marine Ornithology* 27, 1999, pp. 1–12.

Davis, Lloyd S. and John T. Darby, eds. *Penguin Biology.* San Diego: Academic Press, 1990.

De Roy, Tui and Cheryl Lyn Dybas. "The Sheer Wonder of Penguins." *International Wildlife* 21(2), March–April, 1991.

Iwago, Mitsuaki. *Mitsuaki Iwago's Penguins.* San Francisco: Chronicle Books, 1997 (a collection of wildlife photographs).

Hastings, Derek. *Penguins. A Portrait of the Animal World.* New York: Smithmark Publishers, 1997.

Love, John. *Penguins.* Stillwater, Minnesota: Voyageur Press, Inc., 1997.

Müller-Schwarze, Dietland. *The Behavior of Penguins. Adapted to Ice and Tropics.* Albany, New York: State University of New York Press, 1984.

Peterson, Roger Tory. *Penguins.* Boston: Houghton Mifflin Company, 1979.

Reilly, Pauline. *Penguins of the World.* Melbourne: Oxford University Press, 1994.

Schafer, Kevin. *Penguin Planet. Their World, Our World.* Minnetonka, Minnesota: NorthWord Press, 2000.

Sparks, John and Tony Soper. *Penguins.* New York: Facts On File Publications, 1987.

Smith, Roff. "Antarctic Frozen Under." *National Geographic* 200(6), December 2001.

Stonehouse, Bernard. *A Visual Introduction to Penguins.* New York: Checkmark Books, 2000.

Todd, Frank S. *10,001 Titillating Tidbits of Avian Trivia.* Vista: California: Ibis Publishing Company, 1994.

Williams, Tony D. *The Penguins.* Melbourne: Oxford University Press, 1995.

Books for Young Readers

Amato, Carol A. *Penguins of the Galápagos.* Hauppauge, New York: Barron's Educational Series, Inc., 1996.

Bonners, Susan. *A Penguin Year.* New York: Delacorte Press, 1981 (fic).

Chessen, Betsey and Pamela Chanko. *Counting Penguins!* New York; Scholastic, Inc., 1998.

Chester, Jonathan. *A for Antarctica.* Berkeley, California: Tricycle Press, 1995.

Crow, Sandra Lee. *Penguins and Polar Bears. Animals of the Ice and Snow.* Washington, D.C.: National Geographic Society, 1985.

Davis, Lloyd Spencer. *Penguin.* San Diego: Harcourt Brace Jovanovich, 1994.

Jeunesse, Gallimard and René Mettler. *Penguins.* New York: Scholastic, Inc., 1995.

Khanduri, Kamini. *Usborne World Wildlife. Polar Wildlife.* Tulsa, Oklahoma: EDC Publishing, 1992.

McMillan, Bruce. *Puffins Climb, Penguins Rhyme.* San Diego: Harcourt Brace Jovanovich, 1993.

Paladino, Catherine. *Pomona. The Birth of a Penguin.* New York: Franklin Watts, 1991.

Patent, Dorothy Hinshaw. *Looking at Penguins.* New York: Holiday House, 1993.

Pringle, Laurence. *Antarctica. The Last Unspoiled Continent.* New York: Simon & Schuster, 1992.

Soffer, Ruth. *Arctic and Antarctic Life Coloring Book.* Mineola, New York: Dover Publications, Inc., 1998.

Taylor, Barbara. *Eyewitness Books. Arctic and Antarctic.* New York: Alfred A. Knopf, 1995.

Weller, Dave and Mick Hart. *The Changing World. Arctic & Antarctic.* San Diego: Thunder Bay Press, 1996.

Webb, Sophie. *My Season with Penguins. An Antarctic Journal.* Boston: Houghton Mifflin Company, 2000.

Wexo, John Bonnett. *Zoobooks. Penguins.* San Diego: Wildlife Education, Ltd., 1997.

Williams, Geoffrey T. *The Last Frontier. Antarctica.* Los Angeles, Price Stern Sloan, 1992.

Index

hearing, 7
Humboldt penguin, 3, 5, 17, 25, 30, 34, **68**, *69*, 76, 78, 82, 83, 84, 85

I

incubation, general, 21, 26, 30, 31–32, 33
also see individual penguins
IUCN, 82

J

Jackass penguin, see African

K

king penguin, 3, 5, 13, 14, 18, 19, *21*, 24, 26, *26*, 27, 30, 31, 32, 34, **42**, *43*, 83, 85
krill, 19, 44, 46, 48, 50, 52, 54, 56, 60, 70, 76, 79

L

little blue penguin, see fairy
leopard seal, as predator, 44, 77, *77*

M

macaroni penguin, 3, 5, 24, 26, 27, 29, 30, 33, 34, **52**, *53*, 60, 70, 83
Magellanic penguin, 3, 5, *6*, 8, *13*, *14*, 30, 31, 32, **66**, *67*, 68, 83
mating, general, 27–30
also see individual penguins
migration, 17, 34–35
molt, general, 12, 21, 24, 35, *35*
also see individual penguins
mutual display, 29–30

N

name, origin of, 2
nasal glands, 14
nests, 24–26, *24*, 27, 77, 78
also see individual penguins
New Zealand, 5, 9, 54, 56, 58, 50, 62, 64, 78, *77*, 78

O

oil, from penguin fat, 42, 78
oil gland, 13

oil spills, effects of, 60, 78, 81
overfishing, effects on, 79

P

Peruvian penguin, see Humboldt
pollution, effects on, 70, 78
porpoising, *10–11*, 18–19
predators, 4, 7, 17, 19, 34, 60, 62, 72, 76, 77–78, *77*
preening, 13

R

rockhopper penguin, 3, *3*, 5, *20*, 26, 27, 30, 31, 34, *36–37*, **50**, *51*, 77, 83
rookery, 24, 26, *26*
royal penguin, 3, 5, 27, 30, **54**, *55*

S

sight, 7, 20
smell, 7
Snares Island penguin, 3, 5, 30, **60**, *61*
Species Survival Plan, 84
swimming, 7, 15, 17, 18–19, 20

T

temperature, of penguins, 12
temperature control, 13, 14
threatened species, 82, 84

V

vocalizations, 7, 29, 85

W

weight, see individual penguins
wings, see flippers
white-flippered penguin, see fairy

Y

yellow-eyed penguin, 3, 5, 26, 27, 30, **62**, *63*, 70, 78, 79, 85

Goals of the SeaWorld and Busch Gardens Education Departments

Based on a long-term commitment to education, SeaWorld and Busch Gardens strive to provide an enthusiastic, imaginative, and intellectually stimulating atmosphere to help students and guests develop a lifelong appreciation, under-standing, and stewardship for our environment. Specifically, our goals are...

- To instill in students and guests of all ages an appreciation for science and a respect for all living creatures and natural habitats.
- To conserve our valuable natural resources by increasing awareness of the interrelationships of humans and the environment.
- To increase students' and guests' basic competencies in science, math, and other disciplines.
- To be an educational resource to the world.

"For in the end we will conserve only what we love. We will love only what we understand. We will understand only what we are taught."—B. Dioum

Want more information?

If you have a question about animals, call 1-800-23-SHAMU (1-800-237-4268). TDD users call 1-800-TD-SHAMU (1-800-837-4268). These toll-free numbers are answered by the SeaWorld Education Department.

The SeaWorld Education Department has books, teacher's guides, posters, and videos available on a variety of animals and topics. Call or write to request an Education Department Publications brochure or shop online at our e-store.

Visit the SeaWorld/Busch Gardens Animal Information Database at *www.seaworld.org* or *www.buschgardens.org*

E-mail: *shamu@seaworld.org*

Anheuser-Busch Adventure Parks

SeaWorld Orlando
(800) 406-2244
7007 Sea World Drive
Orlando, FL 32821-8097

SeaWorld San Antonio
(210) 523-3606
10500 Sea World Drive
San Antonio, TX 78251-3002

SeaWorld San Diego
(800) 380-3202
500 Sea World Drive
San Diego, CA 92109-7904

Discovery Cove
(877) 434-7268
6000 Discovery Cove Way
Orlando, FL 32821-8097

Busch Gardens Tampa Bay
(813) 987-5555
P.O. Box 9157
Tampa Bay, FL 33674-9157

Busch Gardens Williamsbu
(800) 343-7946
One Busch Gardens Blvd
Williamsburg, VA 23187-878